Poems About

SCH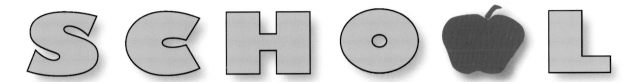OL

BY **America's Children**

EDITED BY Jacqueline Sweeney

Jacqueline Sweeney

BENCHMARK BOOKS

MARSHALL CAVENDISH
NEW YORK

FOR ILGA ZIEMINS-KURENS, WHOSE DEDICATION TO HER ART AND TO THE ART OF HER MANY "CHILDREN" BOTH AMAZES AND HUMBLES ME.

The publisher and editor would like to thank the following schools for opening their doors to us: Alden Place and Elm Drive Elementary Schools (Millbrook Central School District), Amenia and Millerton Elementary Schools (Webutuck School District), Barnum Woods Elementary School (East Meadow Union Free School District), Beekman, LaGrange, and Noxon Road Elementary Schools (Arlington Central School District), Boght Hills and Blue Creek Elementary Schools (North Colonie Central School District), Carrie E. Tompkins Elementary School (Croton-Harmon School District), Central Avenue Elementary School (Mamaroneck Union Free School District), Gardnertown Fundamental Magnet School (Newburgh Enlarged City School District), Germantown Central School (Germantown Central School District), Hackley School, Pawling Elementary and Middle Schools (Pawling Central School District), Scotchtown Avenue School (Goshen Central School District), Tesago Elementary School (Shenendehowa Central School District)

And with thanks to the art teachers (who worked so hard and were so wonderfully supportive): Christine MacPherson, Mary Molloy, Leslie Ann Pesetzky, Carole Pugliese, Mitchell Visoky, Nancy Woogen, Kerry Yankowich, Ilga Ziemins-Kurens

Special thanks to: Miriam Arroyo, Barbara Bortle, Ellen Brooks, Angela Butler, Pat Conques, Dotti Griffin, Anahid Hamparian, Peggy Hansen, Sandy Harvilchuck, Naomi Hill, Carol Ann Jason, Jennifer Lombardo, Mary Lynne Oresen, Joanne Padow, Carol Patterson, Theresa Prairie, Tracy Racicot, Ellen Ramey, Linda Roy, Nicole Sawotka, Jude Smith, Faye Spielberger, Bev Strong, John Szakmary, Glen White, Mary Ellen Whitely

Benchmark Books
Marshall Cavendish
99 White Plains Road
Tarrytown, NY 10591-9001
www.marshallcavendish.com

Text copyright © 2003 by Jacqueline Sweeney
Illustrations copyright © 2003 by Marshall Cavendish Corporation

Book design by Anahid Hamparian

Library of Congress Cataloging-in-Publication Data
Poems about school by America's children / edited by Jacqueline
  Sweeney.
     p. cm. -- (Kids express)
  Summary: Poetry and art by children, describing their social, academic, artistic, and athletic experiences in school.
  ISBN 0-7614-1505-X
  1. Schools--Juvenile poetry. 2. Education--Juvenile poetry.
  3. Children's poetry, American. 4. Children's writings, American.

  [1. Schools--Poetry. 2. American poetry. 3. Children's writings.
  4. Children's art.]   I. Sweeney, Jacqueline. II. Series.
  PS595.S34P64 2002
  811'.6080355--dc21
                         2002002191

Printed in Hong Kong
6   5   4   3   2   1

—Sarah MacLean, *grade 3*

Contents

Teacher's Note

Imagine a classroom full of elementary school children bursting into applause upon hearing an announcement of an upcoming activity. Recess? Lunch? No. Writing poetry! Year after year, this is Jackie Sweeney's effect on students. I have been fortunate enough to witness this phenomenon over the last six years, as Jackie has conducted poetry residencies in the Arlington Central School District.

I study her as she teaches, trying to analyze her strategies. Although I have learned a lot from doing so, there is also some kind of magic at work here. Jackie is a modern-day alchemist, helping students turn their writing into something quite extraordinary.

What does she do? First, she convinces students that they are safe and their ideas are exciting. She focuses on free verse, providing structures through which she introduces students to poetic techniques such as sensory imagery, simile, metaphor, personification, and diction. At the same time, she invites students to surprise her with their own interpretations of these structures. She models extensively with examples from her own imagination and from the work of other students. Her samples are carefully chosen to counteract the notion that poetry treats only butterfly wings and flowers; topics range over every possible subject, from slithering pythons to pestering siblings.

Sensory perceptions are combined in surprising ways. Jackie might begin by asking students to picture a certain color and let it make them feel cold or hot or cool or warm. This is quickly developed into simile as she asks the students to consider how the color (let's say "red") is hot "like what?" As the students come up with their first tentative similes, Jackie immediately gets them to elaborate by asking questions until the child has produced: "Red makes me feel hot like a tomato on a white plate on a picnic table with the sun beating down on it on a summer day." Jackie exclaims, "Now I can see it!" and we are off on another year's excursion into poetry.

Peggy C. Hansen
Noxon Road Elementary School
Poughkeepsie, New York

4

Peter's Pencils

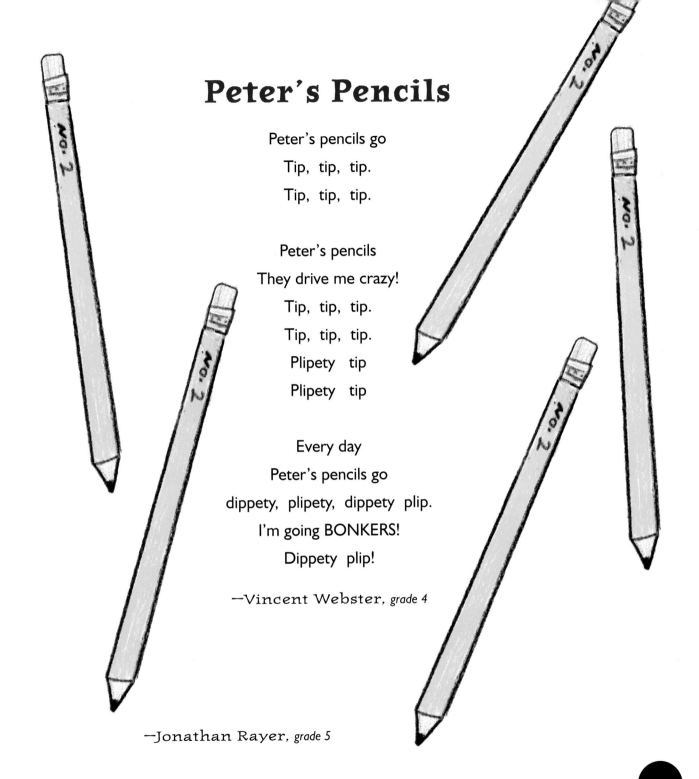

Peter's pencils go
Tip, tip, tip.
Tip, tip, tip.

Peter's pencils
They drive me crazy!
Tip, tip, tip.
Tip, tip, tip.
Plipety   tip
Plipety   tip

Every day
Peter's pencils go
dippety, plipety, dippety plip.
I'm going BONKERS!
Dippety plip!

—Vincent Webster, *grade 4*

—Jonathan Rayer, *grade 5*

Three Wonderful Poems

I

If You Try

I want to do sports but I can't.
I wonder how it feels. I think
it feels like a butterfly. But
I am a caterpillar. Sometime
I'll try and maybe I'll be a butterfly.

II

I Want to be a Teacher

Teachers are smart. I want to
be a teacher. I have to be smart.
You need to study and you'll
finally reach your goal.

III

A Butterfly

A butterfly is beautiful.
Butterflies are amazing.
That's why I want to be a
teacher and I want to be a
butterfly.

—Carlos Luis, *grade 3*

—Anna Ames, *grade 3*

Too Loud!

Loud is not good, especially when a
teacher yells at you. Loud feels pink
when you say the wrong answer.
Loud is good when you are lost
in the dripping blue snow.
Loudness is good to have inside,
because if you were shy
you would barely be noticed.

Hannah is loud like me.
Loud is white if you don't yell
anything—like a hummingbird
that never stops flapping its wings.

Sometimes I am too loud
and get in trouble. "Please,"
I say to my loud side, "You are
too loud!" I wish it could stay,
but when I get in trouble I wish
it would stay away!

—Annette McCormick, *grade 5*

—Michelle Zeliph, *grade 5*

Mrs. Bortle

Mrs. Bortle is like a light blue flower petal on a hot summer day. Sometimes she's like the sun rising at the crack of dawn. She takes me riding down a rainbow. She reminds me of a stampede of cows running across a desert in California! She makes me feel breezy. She is my teacher.

—Megan Montross, *grade 3*

Mr. Baker

You are a sunny day who always cheers me up. Sometimes you're a cloudy day but I know you're still my sunny friend. You take me to a place where all kids are happy. Oh Mr. Baker I always look up to you. You make me feel like a hot tamale on a cold winter day. Nobody's ever made me feel that way.

—Melissa Fuchs, *grade 3*

I Can't Think

My pencil won't write. It keeps on
erasing. When I look at the teacher
it looks like she is going to give
me extra homework. It feels like
I'm a rusted car in a basement.

—Alexander Maruzzella, *grade 3*

The hardest thing
is a three digit number.
It is Math
It is like Money
It is hard
like painting a wall.

—Ezra, *grade 1*

—Chelsea Souter, *grade 4*

The Mouse That Messes Me Up

There is a mouse in my dinner
plate. And I am supposed to eat my
food. I told my mom and she shoved
my face in it. It got in my stomach and
brain. It messes me up in math
and science. And I failed for it!
I wanted to go to Denny's pool.
But now I have to go to summer
school. So then I gave the mouse
cheese and he was never bad again.

—anonymous, *grade 2*

The most lost thing in the world
is my brain during math. It is very
mysterious. It sneaks up
and jumps on you and then you
are at the mercy of the
dark thought.

—Mara, *grade 4*

In Mrs. Hutchings' Head

In Mrs. Hutchings' head
I see a huge list of
teacher-parent conferences
and a big gate leading to her brain.
I climbed over the gate
and a voice said to me
to spell the word
supercalifragilisticexpialidocious
ten times or I would have to
do homework forever!
I got it wrong
and I'm still doing homework today!

—Courtney Miller, *grade 4*

The wind is as cold as winter
I look at the board and
in cursive pink letters I see
MRS. SWEENEY written on
the board. She's coming today. It makes
me feel like 105 kids stampeding through
me. It sounds like hands applauding while a
giant rainbow goes up.

—Sasha Myers-Letusick, *grade 2*

—Sarah MacLean, *grade 3*

Good Grades

I feel proud when I
get good grades like 100s or
like 90s. I feel smart, proud
and I feel really good.
So now I am not scared to
go to school and do math
tests or quizzes. I felt proud
when my 2nd grade teacher
Mrs. Griffin said I am getting
the math. I felt so smart
like I was the smartest kid
in the whole 2nd grade, and
the whole world. I just felt so
great. I love getting good
grades in school.

—Cassandra Milem, *grade 3*

Math

The easiest thing is math. It's like
a piece of cake in my mind. It's like
pure air—like the yellow in the sun.

—Lucas Keasbey, *grade 3*

—Aimee Shevlin, *grade 3*

Embarrassment

Embarrassment is when you get a test back and your friend sees it and laughs about it and tells other people your grade.

—Samantha Cerezo, *grade 5*

Every day at school I get left out. It feels like the sun getting littler and littler.

—Matthew, *grade 3*

—Taylor Davis, *grade 3*

Inside Frustration

Inside frustration is like pressure
pushing in on me. Like pins pushing
against my skin. It sounds silent
except for the pound of my heart.
It's pitch black and I can't see
a thing. It is freezing cold but
also burning hot. It smells sour like
milk going bad. It's still,
and there is nothing moving but my eyes
darting left and right. It feels
like I am floating down in a
bottomless ocean. The air is hard
to breathe and very polluted.
The pressure gets harder and harder
then "POP!"
The frustration ends.

—Shale Breite, *grade 4*

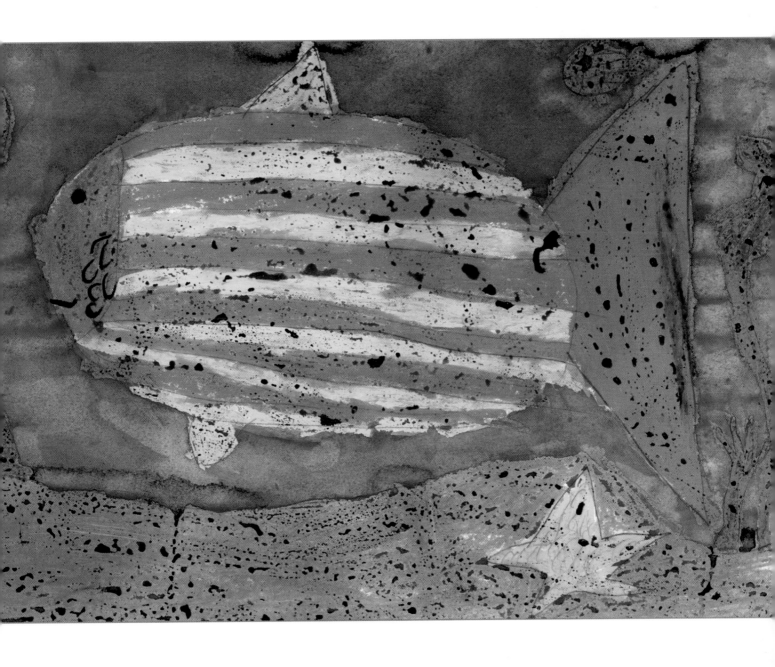

—Gaby, *grade 2*

The Most Boring Day

Sometimes I feel like a caged animal. All
lonely and like my heart is broken. Like my best friend
hates me. The reason is because I have to get out
of this class. It is so boring sitting here while other
people are having fun. I wish it was two days of
school and five days of the weekends.

—Bryan Baldassarri, *grade 5*

Being Stuck

I am a lizard that is stuck
on a window and I can't
come off. I am a piece of
  gum that got stuck on a
big dog's foot and he chewed
  me up. I am a boy that
    got stuck on a test.

—Michael Jordan, *grade 3*

—Jenna Ward, *grade 5*

16

Forgetting

When I forget my best
idea I feel my wheel
stopped and my ideas fell
off. I feel black and
down in the dumps. But
when I remember . . .
I feel green again and
my wheel starts going
again and my cool car
starts driving.

—Danny Goldsmith, *grade 2*

I am blanking. I feel like a
juggler with nothing to juggle or maybe
a tornado with no wind. It is hot because
I feel rushed, and I don't like being
rushed.

—Thomas Oddo, *grade 5*

—Joshua Blumberg, *grade 2*

—William Strayer, *grade 5*

—April Colley, *grade 5*

—Justin Jaggars, *grade 5*

—Sierra Petrone, *grade 5*

Antbill

I am Antbill. I live
in Ant Castle. I am small
but I have an army of
small ants and an army of
small tanks and planes and helicopters
and guns. I can take over a school.

—anonymous, *grade 2*

—Matt Wagner, *grade 2*

Swim Meet Coming

I see myself looking at the paper
that tells me what to do like just
getting back a major grade.
I have to swim 50 fly, 50 breast,
50 back, 50 free and a 100 I.M.
I feel scared to go against
my real teammates like playing
a killing game. This is just
a swim meet for Halloween.

—Christina Hom, *grade 5*

My happiest time was

when I scored
my first goal in roller hockey and my
coach gave me a pink puck.
Pink like a wonderful face.

—Benjamin Nagasing, *grade 3*

—Jake Littman and Anika Rothrock, *grade 3*

Anchored

Being stuck squeezes my brain
like a boa constrictor eating a rat.
It anchors me like a ship would
anchor. It tastes nasty and makes
me sweat like I'm in a
silver metal room with no
window   no door   no secret
passage. Being stuck made
me a poem!

—Tara, *grade 4*

—Brandan Jason, *grade 4*

My scooter is like my life. First I wake
up and feel grouchy and my scooter is still
folded up. I get ready for school. My scooter
is open. I get on the bus and am happy to
see my friends. Now my scooter is doing tricks.
When my scooter falls down and I hurt
myself my day crashes in, but then it's funny
and my day brightens up.

—Christian Calderin, *grade 5*

—Kurt Pope, *grade 2*

Dog Brain

I have a dog in me.
It has a claw like sharp
knives going through
your heart. It smells
like horse manure.
It lives in my brain.
It helps me do better
in math and science and
library and gym. Sometimes
when I'm sleeping it
makes me push the
refrigerator down and makes
me eat one gallon of ice cream.

—Carissa Phillips, *grade 2*

The Breeze in Pottery

Pottery squishes in my hands

like a piece of cheese. It feels like

I've just gotten dirty and I'm taking a bath.

The soft clay between my fingers is

a book, and I'm reading under

a tree at sunset. At first it is small

and bad, but once I start

this colorful project it gets better

and bigger. When I make a pot

so many things are flowing past me.

I'm soaring over a mountain.

Nothing matters, nothing

but the pot.

It's done. Finally I can move

and play. Pots are a part of

my life.

—Emily Arnold, *grade 5*

—Nick Granuzzo, *grade 5*

The Piano

The piano is like a
box that spits out
sound like pots falling
on the floor. The keys
are white as falling
snow. When I play it
I feel lost in dream
land.

—William Brocker, *grade 3*

—Natalie Ruiz, *grade 5*

Make a New World

A guitar is like a heart beating.
It makes a tone like a
baby bee. I take the guitar
play it
and make a new
world.

—Ryan Pease, *grade 3*

—Louie Fortes, *grade 5*

Playing the Piano

Playing the piano is like
feeling for myself as if I
were blind. It's like I'm pushing
on everything I like. Each key
is a different feeling. When I
push the high notes I'm happy.
When I push the low notes I
feel sad sometimes.
The color I see when I play
is black because I imagine
myself in a room with an audience.
When the lights go out it's just
me and the piano. It feels like
it's my best friend because I
can search it and sometimes
it can search me. It sounds
peaceful to me like a
singing bird. I wish I could
be a person who plays
all the time even in school.
It feels so smooth. It makes
me feel special inside.

—Pascale Duvalsaint, *grade 3*

—Cassia Balogh, *grade 5*

29

Art credits

Author index

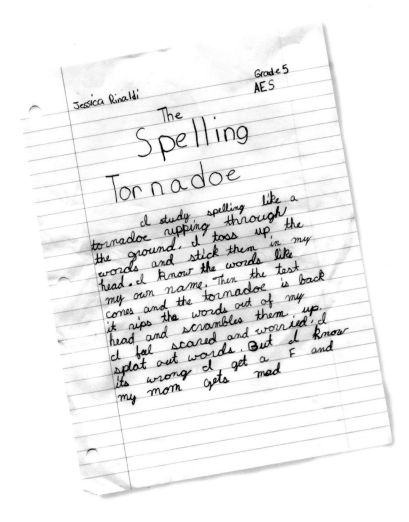

Jessica Rinaldi

The Spelling Tornadoe

I study spelling like a tornadoe ripping through the ground. I toss up the words and stick them in my head. I know the words like my own name. Then the test comes and the tornadoe is back it rips the words out of my head and scrambles them. up. I feel scared and worried. I splat out words. But I know its wrong I get a F and my mom gets mad

—Jessica Rinaldi, *grade 5*